Watercolour Landscape

Watercolour Landscape

JOHN PALMER
& RON RANSON

ANAYA PUBLISHERS LTD
LONDON

First published in Great Britain in 1994 by
Anaya Publishers Ltd., Strode House,
44-50 Osnaburgh Street, London, NW1 3ND.

Managing Editor Miranda Fellows
Art Director Jane Forster
Design Assistant Sarah Willis

British Library Cataloguing in Publication Data

Palmer, John
Watercolour Landscapes. – (Ron Ranson's
Painting School Series)
I. Title II. Ranson, Ron III. Series
751.42

ISBN 1-85470-151-7

Typeset in Plantin in Great Britain by
Litho Link Ltd, Welshpool, Powys, Wales.
Colour reproduction by HBM Print Pte Ltd, Singapore
Printed and bound in Malaysia by Times Offset Ltd

Front Cover: East Anglia
Title Page: Fun of the Fair

Contents

Introduction

RON RANSON

One of the most exciting aspects of my job is finding and writing about artists from all over the world whose work thrills and stimulates me. Every now and again I come across someone, be it in America, Australia, New Zealand or the UK, whose work stops me in my tracks. The first of these was Edward Seago, whose painting had such an affect on me that I changed my career completely and became an artist! Since then I have written about the work of 32 artists worldwide, all of them, to my mind, outstanding.

However, none has given me more pleasure than John Palmer, whose work I discovered on my own doorstep! I am a proud member of the Bristol Savages Club. We paint together in a studio every Wednesday evening and it was at one of these sessions that I first saw John's work. The looseness and distinction of his style astounded me. I had never seen anyone else draw and paint in this way, combining delicate pencil drawing with wild, loose watercolour washes. You would not expect this combination to work, but the results are truly thrilling.

A thoroughly modest, self-effacing man, John is constantly surprised by the admiration his work commands. Although he has held many exhibitions and his paintings fetch high prices, as well as having been reproduced in other people's books, he had never considered producing a book himself. As Series Editor

of 'Ron Ranson's Painting School', part of my brief was to select the artists I felt best suited to each particular title in the series. For the third book in the series, 'Drawing and Sketching', I knew that John's work would be ideal, if only I could persuade him to do it. Modest as he is, he expressed doubts, but was finally persuaded and the result was a book which I consider to be a little masterpiece. Having got him going, I did not want to let go, and talked him into producing the illustrations for Watercolour Landscape.

We decided not to create another beginners' 'how to do it' book, rather Watercolour Landscape is a more advanced volume, directed towards the reader who has mastered the basic crafts of watercolour painting and who is now looking for an injection of inspiration and guidance to progress further. We also wanted to suggest new sources of subject matter and get away from the mundane, enlarging the whole concept of watercolour landscape. To take one example, we have looked at the field of sport, which offers endless opportunities for the artist. We want you, the reader, to look at landscape with a new eye.

The first half of this book will help you with more professional ways of working and picture design – a subject rarely covered in painting books. We hope that the second half will freshen your approach and give you new ideas for subject matter.

John used a combination of techniques which you will be introduced to in more detail later on in the book. First he laid a wash over the paper. Next, mixing pencil and watercolour media, he created a pattern of woodland across the composition. The placing of the trees makes for an interesting design.

JOHN PALMER

Each art book has its own set of challenges. When using watercolour, the limitations of the medium encourage me to explore the techniques available and manipulate them to achieve my desired effects – sometimes even working against the rules! I have collaborated with Ron at various stages in the development of this project, both of us inspiring and pushing one another along with ideas and techniques, almost on a competitive basis. I used to work in a large commercial studio alongside 30 other artists. Now that I work independently I miss their camaraderie and humour. Working with Ron recreated something of that atmosphere, the buzz of ideas and the opportunity to compare our efforts as we went along. I valued Ron's opinions and assessments, whether favourable or otherwise!

Watercolour Landscape guided me into new territories where I discovered the excitement of working with a greater range of effects, experimenting with patterns, colours, reshaping paintings in the studio, on occasions with the minimum effort to gain maximum effect, sometimes just floating the colour on the paper, allowing the pigment to move in its own directions and do the work for me.

On many of the illustrations, the watercolour has

These two paintings show the versatility with which John approaches the subject of landscape.

The wide, verdant landscape, Warren Farm, left, demonstrates a traditional viewpoint and conventional application of the watercolour medium.

In the painting, Pecking Order, below, John chooses to consider a more detailed composition and a humorous narrative to enhance the scene.

been little more than a support, enhancing line work with delicate washes. On others it has been used almost impasto, giving a vigorous intense result, accentuated by the use of brushwork.

Failures have been as important as the successes, those painting we decided not to include in the final selection teaching me as many important lessons as those which appear. The confidence to be spontaneous and fresh will always be reflected in the final results. Watercolour provides you with the opportunity to let the moment take over, courting success or disaster, when it works there is no other medium quite like it.

WAYS OF WORKING

In this book we are assuming that you have already gained the basic skills of the watercolour craft. Until you can use your materials with a degree of ease and familiarity, you can go no further. However, once you do feel confident with watercolour, you are ready to move on to the next challenge. This is to build on what you have learned and progress to a more professional standard of work which goes beyond mere technical efficiency, important though that is.

Our intention is to help you make that leap forward, to produce work which is well-designed and stamped both with authority and your own personality. The first vital step is more mental than physical, as you must learn to think about the design of your picture before you start painting, rather than trusting to luck once you have actually got going. This takes mental strength as well as self-discipline, as the desire to jump straight into a painting seems to be a universal failing. In fact I believe it to be the main factor that keeps amateur painters in their place – as amateurs!

In this painting, John has achieved a balance between formality and freedom. He painted an initial neutral beige-grey wash. Once dry he took a large 2in brush and applied random washes of yellow ochre and blue-grey across the top two thirds of the painting, creating a moody atmosphere. In contrast, he then used stippling and semi-dry brushwork to create angular shapes in the foreground.

When planning this image, John used a black and white photograph of the scene for reference, ignoring most of the details but preserving the vertical tree. Although to some degree abstract, the image of the tree firmly roots the painting in reality.

Composition

CENTRE OF INTEREST

As beginners, we start simply by painting what is in front of us to the best of our ability, but in order to make a more personal statement you have to get away from purely recording a scene and advance into the 'reality of composition'. You may need to move some of the objects in front of you or even reject them altogether, to form a better composition, which in turn will infinitely improve the quality of your painting. In order to make these judgements, you must first learn the principles of design. You must form harmony out of the glorious chaos of nature to make your work pleasing to the eye. Nature only provides the raw material – your task is to reassemble it in a skilful arrangement on a flat piece of paper.

Just what are the principles of design? Basically they are a set of common sense rules, which you have to absorb and learn to apply automatically. The watchwords to remember are unity, dominance, balance, contrast, gradation and harmony. We all have a basic need for unity and order, and in art this is best achieved by the use of another of the principles – dominance – something which is more important than anything else in a painting. It could be the brightest colour, the largest object or the strongest contrast – the first thing that hits your eye when you look at a painting. There must be no doubt about this.

The worst thing you can possibly do is have two

Above, the small sketch illustrates placing the centre of interest to the top left-hand side of the composition. The triangular shape of the mountain is emphasised by the weight of colour.

Left, the larger sketch shows the middle distance dominated by a line of buildings drawing the eye to the centre. Windsor Castle is placed just off centre to create balance.

equal objects vying for attention. Unity is achieved by linking everything else around the dominant feature in a cohesive way. This feature is known as the centre of interest, and should be the reason for wanting to paint a particular scene in the first place. If you like, it is the star of the show, and everything around it must support it or be eliminated. Obviously, where we put this object is of prime importance, ideally the distance from it to all sides of the painting should be of a different dimension.

The worst crime is to have your centre of interest bang in the middle of the paper. This probably sounds obvious, but it is easily forgotten when you sit down on site. Perhaps you are painting in a wood surrounded by equally-sized or shaped trees. The secret here is to make one tree dominant over the rest, making it larger than the others, or more contrasting. This will require conscious and creative thought on your part.

Another way to make your centre of interest quite clear, is to provide a pathway for the eye to follow which positively invites it into the picture and then guides it to your chosen feature. This could be a river, a road or even the curve of a shoreline. It should not be too abrupt, but must give the eye time to appreciate the whole picture before arriving at its final destination. This concept shouldn't be regarded as vague theory but must be applied to every picture that you plan and paint.

Above, in this sketch the centre of interest is achieved by the activity of the gate leading the eye into the picture from the bottom left.

Right, the composition is emphasised by the use of strong colours, split horizontally into three sections. The blue sky draws the eye to the centre of interest, the building, which is counterbalanced by the telegraph pole and wires leading away into the distance.

BALANCING GROUPS

Balance in a painting is visual comfort. If a picture is out of balance it makes us feel uncomfortable just to look at it. There are two kinds of balance in a painting – formal and informal. Formal is where you place something in the centre of a painting or have two objects of equal weight on either side, with a central axis. This can be visually boring and on the whole is not to be recommended. Informal balance is, on the whole, far more attractive, and is best explained by using the example of a see-saw. If an adult sits on one end of the see-saw and a child on the other it will be badly balanced. If, however the adult moves towards the centre and the child remains on the other end, informal balance is achieved. In a painting, a dark object appears heavier than a light-toned one, so that a small dark shape can be balanced by a larger light one.

When deciding how to group elements within a painting, therefore, the principle of balance must be adhered to. Planning how groups will be integrated into your composition must be carried out at the preliminary stages. Use each element as a tool in the manufacture of your design idea – it can make the creative process far more challenging and the end result really quite individual.

Animals can form an important part of the overall design of a picture, for example, and can become an integral part of the pattern if they are incorporated into the initial stages and not simply added as an appendage at the end. Like human figures, they must be handled in the same style as the rest of the painting.

Grouping elements can create an excellent focal point in a painting; whether a flock of sheep, a herd of cows or a group of buildings. A flock of seagulls on one side of a picture, for example, will balance up and complement a group of static boats on the other side, while their formation will add flow and movement to your design.

It is important to counterchange any group within a painting against a contrasting background. Light sheep or cows against dark trees or dark animals against light skylines are good examples of how to create a sense of balance and harmony in the grouping of elements across your painting.

Left, a group of buildings nestling into the hillside form a natural triangle. The left-hand side of the composition is left clear to emphasise the structures and their height.

Below, to break up what was otherwise a flat composition, John added a flock of seagulls at the end of the painting process. They enliven the scene, linking land to sky.

Left, groupings of sheep form a pattern, one mass to the left hand-side, and then separated to the right. This creates an informal balance against the distant trees which curve around the horizon. John has deliberately worked in monochrome to achieve a harmonious composition.

UNIFYING ELEMENTS

You might not be conscious of the fact, but when you look at a painting you will judge its merit on whether or not the image is unified. The worst types of paintings are those which display a scattered collection of separate objects without any visual linkage, and no interlocking shape or tone. No matter how well individual parts are painted, if there is no cohesive quality to a work it will fail.

It is vital not to put one colour, texture or value in only one part of the painting. If you do your painting will immediately become disjointed. A spot of bright orange on a roof should be repeated, however minutely, somewhere else on the picture surface. In any picture nothing must happen just once.

In order to create a unified composition it is essential to select the most suitable viewpoint. If you choose which angle to paint a scene from at random

you will be making the chances of producing a cohesive image less likely. Make preliminary tonal sketches to test out the chosen view.

Positioning the actual elements within the scene is important too. For example, if you have a foreground gate, don't repeat it in the distance directly above on the paper. You could repeat it horizontally, but it would be even more effective if you repeated it obliquely. The same applies to strong colour, this too should be echoed rather than repeated.

All this planning must be done beforehand in preliminary sketches. You simply can't design a painting as you go along, there are too many other decisions to make at that stage. Professionals always do their preliminary work beforehand. Not so most amateurs who think it is a waste of time and paper and always want to start directly on their finished painting. Perhaps that is what keeps them amateurs!

In order to select a viewpoint it is often of value first to make two or three sketches of the same scene but from different positions. First John made two sketches of the view. One looks over the river from the vantage point of the castle. For the other he moved down and painted the opposite view, from the riverbank. Finally, he made a large painting of a general view of the city, taking all of its elements into account in this more complex composition.

TONAL CONTRAST

As an artist you must think of yourself primarily as an entertainer. The last thing you want to do is bore your audience. So, the next two things we should consider are gradation and contrast. They both have strong entertainment value, by changing from one extreme to the other, but they do it in different ways.

Take contrast: this is an abrupt change from cool to warm, light to dark or large to small. This technique must be used with restraint, preferably around the focal point, as it attracts immediate attention. An important word to remember in this context is counterchange – the placing of a dark object or area immediately adjacent to a light one. This can be used creatively by making a post or tree trunk light against a dark background, but changing it to dark as soon as it reaches the light sky.

This device can be used universally throughout a painting, without the viewer being aware of it. Taking this concept further, you can, for example, deliberately put a dark tree behind the corner of a house to throw up the lighter roof more dramatically.

Left, three colour sketches show how diverse watercolour is as a tonal medium. The colour of each of the initial washes in the sketches has dictated the atmosphere of the ensuing scenes: an avocado-coloured wash enhances a sombre winter evening where light bounces off the loch. A pale blue wash acts as a complementary to the rich orange hues of autumn. The sultry heat of high summer as evening closes in is accentuated by the underlying peach wash.

Above, in this painting the colours are kept to a limited tonal range. The patchwork of towns, fields, hills and sky appear through the tonal washes, fragmented by essential areas of white paper but also linked together by pencil marks.

GRADATION

Gradation, on the other hand, is a much more subtle and gradual change, reflecting many natural effects on the landscape. The paint lends itself well to gradual changes in tone, and by creating a graduated wash, either of tonal variation in one colour, or through a series of compatible hues, you will create the basis for a subtle and atmospheric landscape, perhaps of dawn breaking over rolling plains, or night falling over rocky mountains.

Flat surfaces can change slowly in colour from warm to cool or from dark to light, avoiding monotony. Foregrounds, too, should vary in this way. Gradation of tone across a shape or large area is just as important. It is particularly useful in the case of uneventful areas such as skies or foregrounds.

This is one of the distinguishing factors which separate accomplished painters from beginners who paint logically but unimaginatively. This is a shame, since gradation can make a huge difference to the overall quality of your painting.

Left, four methods of painting graduated washes, from top down: lightening towards the centre, deepening towards the centre, creating a dark band against a paler wash, working from bottom to top and from dark to light.
Right, gradation is subtle in variation across the paper.

PRACTICE

○ To avoid the paint furring down the paper, tilt it sideways and diagonally while working so the watercolour floods in all directions.

○ Watercolour washes have a habit of drying much lighter than you might imagine, so ensure that your paint mix holds enough pigment to achieve the colour intensity you were planning. It is worth testing colour intensity on a piece of rough paper before applying it to a final painting to check its strength. Of course you will need to wait for it to dry first!

These three illustrations demonstrate just some of the devices which you can use to lead the eye right through the picture.

Left, the curved path takes the eye towards the horizon, and is enhanced by the contrast in colour on either side of its curve.

Bottom left, the sweep of land and snow make a natural guide for the eye from foreground to woodland in the distance.

Right, utilising texture as a visual device, John has spattered watercolour over a dry wash to draw the eye from the foreground through to the castle settling on the horizon.

Above, the actual angles of the buildings and the path naturally bisect and divide the illustration, vertically, horizontally and diagonally. A combination of pencil and flat washes create textures and line to add depth and interest to the scene. John used stippling discreetly to enhance the luminosity of the watercolour washes in the foliage to the left of the footpath, which in turn leads the eye into the heart of the painting. Mixing watercolour with other media, such as pastel, oil pastel or coloured pencil may add texture and depth.

Top, the image is divided both by the natural geography of water and land on the vertical, which John enhances by tonal contrast. This unusual composition shows just how imaginative the landscape can be as subject!

Above, a low horizon divides the landscape, giving greater value to the sky which seems to overwhelm the landscape below.

HARMONY, TONE, ABSTRACTION

Harmony appeals to most of us, in all walks of life and is another principle which we need to use in our painting. It is not difficult to achieve once you are aware and begin to think about it as an integral aspect of landscape composition.

When we talk about harmony in colour, we are referring to the adjacent colours in the colour wheel. The harmonies of green would be blue-green or perhaps yellow-green. If you think about red, you will quickly see that the harmonious colours are purple-reds or oranges. Harmony is also applied to shape, for instance a circle and an oval are harmonious. Turning to value, the harmonic of a dark tone is another which is slightly darker or lighter than the first.

One of the most difficult principles to explain, but one which is of vital importance, is the use of tonal pattern. Tone occurs in any colour and is the lightness and darkness of a colour. Imagine white paper as 0 going up to 100% with black. Beginners are inevitably afraid of this vast scale and tend to stick in a comfort zone, at about 45-50%. As a result, their paintings look flat and rather boring. Usually my first task in my classes is to force my students to use this whole scale of tones by restricting them to using one colour only.

Once you have achieved a full range of tones, you have to learn to place them within your painting to form an overall pattern. For the sake of simplicity, let us just think of them as lights, darks and mid-tones. It is not a simple thing to do if you have never seen it done before, but without this skill you will never become a competent painter in any medium.

On the whole, the stronger and more powerful the pattern, the better the result, but a representational landscape cannot be achieved at the same time as you are actually painting a final work. You must plan your patterns beforehand if you are to create a painting which feels complete. The time taken for this preparation is never wasted. American watercolourist Ed Whitney spoke words of wisdom when he stated,

John painted this landscape in a one-off session, by dampening various areas of the paper and using one large decorator's brush to apply undiluted pigment fast and loose.

'You should design like a tortoise and paint like a hare'. Professionals know this and would never think of beginning their painting without preparatory work. Amateurs often think it is a waste of time and paper, and just want to get on with a finished picture. Then they wonder why their composition does not have the strength and unity they had hoped to achieve.

Experimenting with pattern in the landscape, by freeing yourself of the visual constraints of representation can also be a rewarding exercise. The landscape is made up of patterns of colour, light, tone and movement. Play with these elements on your paper, freeing the watercolour to dictate the pattern which emerges, as John often does. Look at the actual details of a landscape scene: the sun shimmering over water, the rough surface of rocks adjacent to a cool blue sky, ploughed earth next to a soft, grassy verge. Pick up on these elements and create patterns which reflect their colours and textures in your final work.

TECHNIQUES

If you make your pattern too consistent across the composition you will be in danger of creating a monotonous picture. If, on the other hand, you strive to attain too varied or colourful a pattern, you might well sacrifice harmony and balance.

Mix the landscape's colours and wash them individually onto the relevant areas on the paper, allowing them to flood into one another to add sparkle and freedom to your work. Once you have allowed the colours to swim freely across the paper, you can add final details. John often works in this way. He will apply the watercolour washes in a free and random manner. Once they are completely dry, he will add detail in pencil over the top. In a landscape this might consist of features such as buildings or trees. He may then enhance the final composition with bright touches of oil pastel or pen and ink.

John has wet areas of the paper and applied the pigment to it. The dampness reacts with the paint to create interesting granular effects. On occasion, the bristles of the hog hair brush have added further texture. Although this is an abstract image, John has determined to maintain a degree of structure. Note the importance of the areas left white and the bold directions of the brushstrokes in the foreground.

John selected abstract details from two works which he felt best emphasised an aspect of the particular landscape. The first, of a textured rock face, takes advantage of the NOT surface of the watercolour paper and John's subsequent spatter work, scumbling and wash formation. The second concentrates on the tonal qualities of a tree trunk and branches.

Working on Location

I positively enjoy the social aspect of painting in the open air. For some reason artists are trusted and people feel quite safe to come up and chat to you while you work. But painting in public can come as quite a shock to the system, and brings with it all kinds of problems – both practical and aesthetic! For some people, the very idea of painting out in the open, under the scrutiny of passers-by, terrifies them. You have to learn to discourage too much conversation, otherwise you will never get any work done. An occasional grunt is often perfectly satisfactory for adults and a broad smile for children. If you do feel self-conscious, break yourself in gently. Instead of launching straight into a full-scale painting, start by sketching in some secluded location. Sketches alone make invaluable reference material for your later return to the sanctity of the studio.

If you spend some time working on location, it will show in your work as you will be confronting your subject directly, making notes, picking up reference materials, watching the effects of light and weather conditions, the time of day, the change in seasons.

The fresh spirit of the landscape can be thoroughly captured by watercolour when working out of doors.

One of the first lessons the painter en plein air must grasp is the importance of tonal sketches! Never leave home without a pencil and sketchbook within which to make these preliminary marks.

TONAL SKETCHES

When you are working on location a sketch pad and pencils are invaluable. A two or three minute tonal sketch will immediately show you whether the painting is worth doing. It will concentrate your mind acutely on the subject, making sure you have one object of interest, properly emphasised and supported. It will also show you whether or not the tonal pattern is strong and the design well-balanced. And most importantly, that every element is interlocked with the rest of the picture.

Do at least four of these before you get your paints out. By this time you will know which of your subjects have worked and which are not worth bothering about, so saving yourself sheets of expensive watercolour paper and hours of disappointing work. As you persevere with this method you will wonder how you ever managed without it.

So, to the practice of making tonal sketches. You need a good sketch pad of cartridge paper and a pencil. Ignore the H6s and HBs, they are useless for what you want to do. You will need anything from 2B to 6B, which will enable you to achieve a good tonal range. Remember that what we are talking about here is tone and not line. Unfortunately we are taught at school to put lines around everything. I call them wires, and the first tonal sketches are usually abysmal. You must learn first to use the side of your pencil, not the point, and get into the habit of varying the pressure on your pencil. When writing, you only use one pressure but

in these sketches you need to use from half an ounce to half a pound, in order to get the full range from the palest grey to pitch black.

Always begin your sketch by drawing a rectangle in proportion to your finished painting, but never more than 2×3ins. Avoid at all costs attempting to put detail into the sketch. You are not drawing objects, you are drawing shapes or areas of tone. Concentrate on producing the overall pattern in miniature. You need only take two or three minutes on each one but from it you will be able to visualise the way your finished painting will look. Be self-critical, try at least two or three and make them look simple but exciting.

The time you spend on your tonal sketches really is vital. It will save wasted paper and you will learn to reject a poor design with too many bitty shapes at this early stage. Once you are satisfied with your design, you will begin your painting with more confidence. Many of the principles which we have already covered: unity, domination and balance, should also be incorporated into your tonal sketch.

When you are doing these sketches on site, a good trick is to screw up your eyes until you can only just see through them. This will eliminate all detail and enable you to see the actual tones quite distinctly. With your eyes open you almost see too much!

Once you have achieved the perfect tonal sketch, it then has to be turned into a full colour picture. This transition seems to worry and confuse students, as they attempt to apply the tonal principles to colours.

Top far left: 2B pencil is applied over a dried wash of pale ochre.

Bottom far left: brown wax crayon is applied over a dried wash of pale ochre.

Middle: brown coloured pencil over a pale sienna wash of pale sienna.

Top left: black pen and smudged ink are applied over a dried wash of pale ochre.

Bottom left: grey oil pastel over a dried wash of pale grey.

However, take heart and remember that tone is simply the lightness and darkness of any colour, regardless of hue. I find that one of the best ways of proving whether my colour picture has worked is to photostat it. If it is right, then the picture will still work perfectly well in black and white.

Let me make a final plea here for you to persevere with these tonal sketches. Don't imagine you can bypass them. They will make a difference!

CAPTURING THE SPIRIT OF THE LANDSCAPE
Once you are satisfied with your original sketch, and not until then, you are in a position to get your paints out and reproduce your design idea in soft pencil on your watercolour paper. Make sure that your sketch is in front of you and refer to it constantly. It is so easy, while concentrating on your actual painting, to lose sight of your original design. This applies to work in

A small tonal sketch using pastel pencil denotes the shape and tonal qualities of the scene, which is painted up later on in the studio, using wash and dry brush techniques.

A tonal study in oil pastel on a dried pale ochre wash again plans the composition and tonal qualities. John painted the wash before he went out on location, so that it would be dry and ready for the oil pastel to be sketched onto once he had found his subject. The completed painting denotes variegated washes painted onto dry watercolour paper to take advantage of the backruns which this technique produces. All pencil work was done before John began painting, enabling him to plan a detailed composition from his initial rough.

the studio as well as on location. Students often find that, although their tonal sketch was arresting and exciting, though only three inches wide, the final painting somehow got watered down and became dull and ordinary, lacking colour and sparkle. Often this is because they have been unable to translate their black and white tones into colour – something which can easily be learned. With the subject before you on location and your tonal sketches to hand, practice should make for lively results.

In your first design sketch, put in the main shapes and pattern without getting carried away with fiddly detail. However, in a finished painting you can be seduced into putting cracks in doors and bricks in walls or even every leaf on a tree. It is a hard habit to break, but try to capture that first feeling of excitement and stick to the simplicity of concept. Make sure that your audience can do some of the work themselves. They also have imagination and will enjoy using it.

LOOKING FOR LOCATIONS

Let's imagine we are actually out on location, looking for subjects. So many of us seem to travel long distances searching for the perfect viewpoint, ignoring more mundane subjects like field gates or bends in lanes. Rather than trying to find the perfect panorama, look closely at the details within the landscape which might capture the spirit of the location. A single well-lit tree or gate might seem a simplistic subject but scenes like these can make beautiful images and show a sensitivity and understanding by you towards your surroundings.

We want also to avoid the picture postcard type scene, and search for a more unusual and subtle viewpoint, and perhaps more exciting lighting conditions. You have a better chance of getting your work accepted for exhibitions with an unusual subject than the mundane. A picture of a fallen tree in the middle of a wood, with dramatic lighting and composition, for example, can be strong and exciting when put in the right hands – in contrast, a thatched cottage in a cosy landscape is extremely hard to make original. You would have to be a superb painter to get that past a selection committee for a show!

You can also learn a lot by painting on location with another artist. It is amazing what a fellow painter will notice that you have missed, even though you may have painted in that place a hundred times before. To succeed you have to be turned on by a subject. When this happens the hair on the back of your neck will

The two sketches are done in preparation for the final painting. First, HB pencil is sketched over a prepared background of pale ochre wash to create the composition and the grouping of the buildings against the landscape. The colour sketch enables John to consider the atmosphere of the scene by simplifying areas into colour patterns.

In the finished painting, the preliminary sketch has given John the confidence to work in broad strokes, once again simplifying the scene and unifying the image with general washes across the surface of the paper.

PRACTICE

○ Travel light! Remember that each watercolour, in different stages of solution, will create a variety of hues. Just take three colours, perhaps a red, yellow and blue. By reducing your range you will improve your understanding of colour variation.

○ You only need take two brushes on location – one broad and one pointed. Chinese brushes are good alternatives to more traditional watercolour brushes. They can be used to create both very fine and broad marks and washes. This versatility may well be of benefit when you are travelling light.

Spending a little time working on the spot, John created three different interpretations of the harbour scene: the general scene, a close-up of the harbour and boats, the pattern of the buildings. This enabled him to analyse every aspect of the scene and gain a firm impression of the subject. As a result, the finished painting is done with speed and confidence. His familiarity with the subject enables John to concentrate on the more abstract qualities of light across the water and buildings.

stand up and you know that the adrenalin will be transferred to the paper.

When you get down to painting in the landscape, remember where you are! Many amateurs spend 90% of their time looking down at the paper, occasionally glancing up at the subject to refuel. The British artist John Yardley and I sometimes paint together and I have noticed that he will study his subject carefully, constantly referring to it as he works. In fact he probably spends more time looking than he does painting, just putting down an occasional stroke on his paper. Study the subject carefully as you work, allowing your eye to flicker up to consider the scene then down to make a mark. A fast stroke is often much more exciting than a slow one, and by taking extra time looking you are more likely to create inspired watercolours.

DESIGN RULES

It is surprising to see that even the most experienced artists, when they get out on location, are often so engrossed in capturing the scene and coping with the weather conditions that they forget many of the rules of composition. They may even commit the cardinal sin of painting the horizon half way up the picture. One of the first things to do is decide whether the sky is your dominant feature, in which case you will place your horizon low and concentrate on the cloud effects. However, if you want to emphasise some other features in the landscape, such as barns, trees and hills, you must keep the horizon high with a minimum of sky. If this is the case, keep the sky close in tone to the landscape to avoid too great a contrast.

Remember, too that other important design rule: domination. For instance, in a sky scene, one cloud should dominate. One feature in the landscape should always be given dominance even if nature hasn't provided you with it. It is your job as an artist to enhance the scene in front of you, not copy it!

Editing nature can be fun. Don't feel that you have to copy every nuance, every tree, every bush. You have the creative freedom to respond in any way you so choose. And another thing, if you wish to create a painting which appears balanced and harmonious, you may well consciously want to leave out a lot of the elements spread before you – or even add some which weren't really there!

Another design rule – unity – will be achieved by treating all of the elements in a picture in the same style, be it sky, distance or foreground. This applies to figures too. Putting a tight figure into an otherwise loose landscape will ruin it.

The overall view of the landscape is considered from a variety of stances by the artist. John has selected a high viewpoint, a low viewpoint, a distant view of the hills and a more detailed composition including the church. In each case, he has edited nature to suit his needs; simplifying the scene, adding cows, trees and using tonal variation to create different moods.

Above, working in windy conditions you must have your wits about you! Once you have established your position, try to capture the essence of the moment. This rapid, angular line illustration accentuates the lean of the trees against the wind. The horizon level is kept low to emphasise the conditions.

Below, John made this rapid sketch moments before the heavens opened and soaked him to the skin! He used a combination of undiluted pigment and washes, making additional marks with the other end of the brush to add tension – before running for cover!

WEATHER EFFECTS

The seasons and weather conditions have an important affect when you are working on location. Each has its own charm – as well as possible downfalls. As a watercolourist, extremes of heat and cold will affect the drying speed of your paint. Let's take these problems one at a time. In the heat of summer, in the Greek Islands, Southern Spain, Florida or Australia, you will face the same difficulties. Try, wherever possible, to avoid painting in direct sunlight. Always find a bit of shade to paint under. Otherwise, when you get home, your painting will look washed out, as the direct sunlight will affect your tonal judgment. Overcome quick-drying by putting more water onto the paper at the beginning of the process or by painting in a more staccato fashion than you might normally. Shadows are also important to balance against bright areas of full sunlight. It is probably best to leave them until the end and then to put them in

TECHNIQUES

A soft pencil will give you a greater range of tonal effects for sketching out of doors, capable of both soft and hard lines. Also, use it to make notes on the colours in the landscape. Take a variation of coloured papers or ready–prepared washes for making colour notes on site. If you have not preselected the subject for a location painting, take a variety of prepared tone grounds – perhaps some subtle washes of raw sienna or pale ochre, as well as some more vibrant washes of green, blue or pink.

Below, this snow scene was virtually completed with one wash, mixing the rich reds as a foil to the starkness of the snow. When dry, John added the foliage with a dry brush.

Below, the atmosphere has determined the colours and style of this painting. Controlled within a limited tonal range, John has created an intense response to a light-infused landscape.

Right, Ayre's Rock by contrast is shown in early evening light, the shadows drawn long against the landscape and the tonal range more diverse. The band of blue sweeping across the skyline complements the arid red foreground and intensifies the heat of the scene.

quickly and decisively with the minimum of fuss. If you add shadows gradually their directions will have changed by the time you have finished.

In high winds there is alway the danger that your easel could blow over! To avoid this, fasten a piece of cord to the centre with a slip knot at the other end. Then, before starting to paint, find a suitable rock to put in the slip knot to act as a weight. Sometimes though, you can note the wind direction and find a suitable wall for protection. In mist conditions the air is heavy with moisture and you will be able to cut down on the amount of water you apply to the paper. The slow drying can be a positive advantage for achieving a misty effect!

Rain, can be quite the most difficult condition to paint in. Even worse is showery weather, and you must be prepared to turn your board over the instant you feel the first spot of rain or your painting will be ruined. While for most of us rain spots are a disaster, John manages to capitalise on them in his paintings!

If you are planning a painting trip anywhere icy your main problem will be numb fingers. Try to paint the main washes with gloves on, just taking them off for more detailed work. Always wait, if possible, for any falling snow to stop and the sun to come out. Then you get really exciting contrasts of shadow and light. Possibly the easiest condition to work in is when it is bright but with overcast skies. The light remains constant over a long period. The light on your paper too will remain constant.

EQUIPMENT

Finally, a word about your equipment – keep it to the absolute minimum, which should enable you to carry it under one arm. A sure sign of a beginner is one who staggers around with far too much, dropping bits and pieces on the way. Like an experienced traveller, dispense with any unnecessary gear.

A limited bag of paints and paper can make painting on location even more of an adventure. By cutting down on your colour or brush options you will have to experiment with the colours you have to hand. Watercolour can be mixed and applied in so many ways that any one colour can do a variety of jobs. And using only a limited palette can also make harmony and unity come more easily.

PRACTICE

○ Don't try and interpret too complicated a scene – watercolour does not lend itself to highly detailed outdoor sketching.

○ Make a note of the shadow directions when you start working on a scene – otherwise you will lose all sense of the light in your work as it changes throughout the day.

○ Rather than attempting to convey the dramatic light and shade contrasts in the landscape as they change throughout the day, concentrate only on one particular moment which you have captured in a preliminary sketch.

One of the best reasons for working out on location is to gather reference material to be used later in the studio for your finished painting. Make notes about the time of day, light source, weather conditions, smells and sounds to refresh your memory. Also, many artists find that taking photographs can help them regain their first impressions. Pick up pieces of heather, wood, grass, even earth, if it will be a useful aid in the studio.

Remember always to ask permission before painting on private land, don't trample over growing crops, keep to the footpaths and don't leave gates gaping open. Of course any litter should be taken home with you, not left for some unsuspecting animal to eat!

I hope that I haven't put you off painting on site. It is worth braving the elements and many artists find that their best paintings are produced in the open air. The very difficulties seem to sharpen the mind and intellect and the sounds and smells all around stimulate the creative impulse. So, do get out there, work quickly, avoid a laborious approach, and above all, enjoy yourself!

Above, a bright sketch to reflect the nature of the summer's day contrasts, right, with a less balmy occasion. Painted from the same viewpoint, John responds to a dramatic downpour which lasted for a matter of minutes. Immediacy of response was essential, in fact this could definitely be described as a reflex painting!

In the Studio

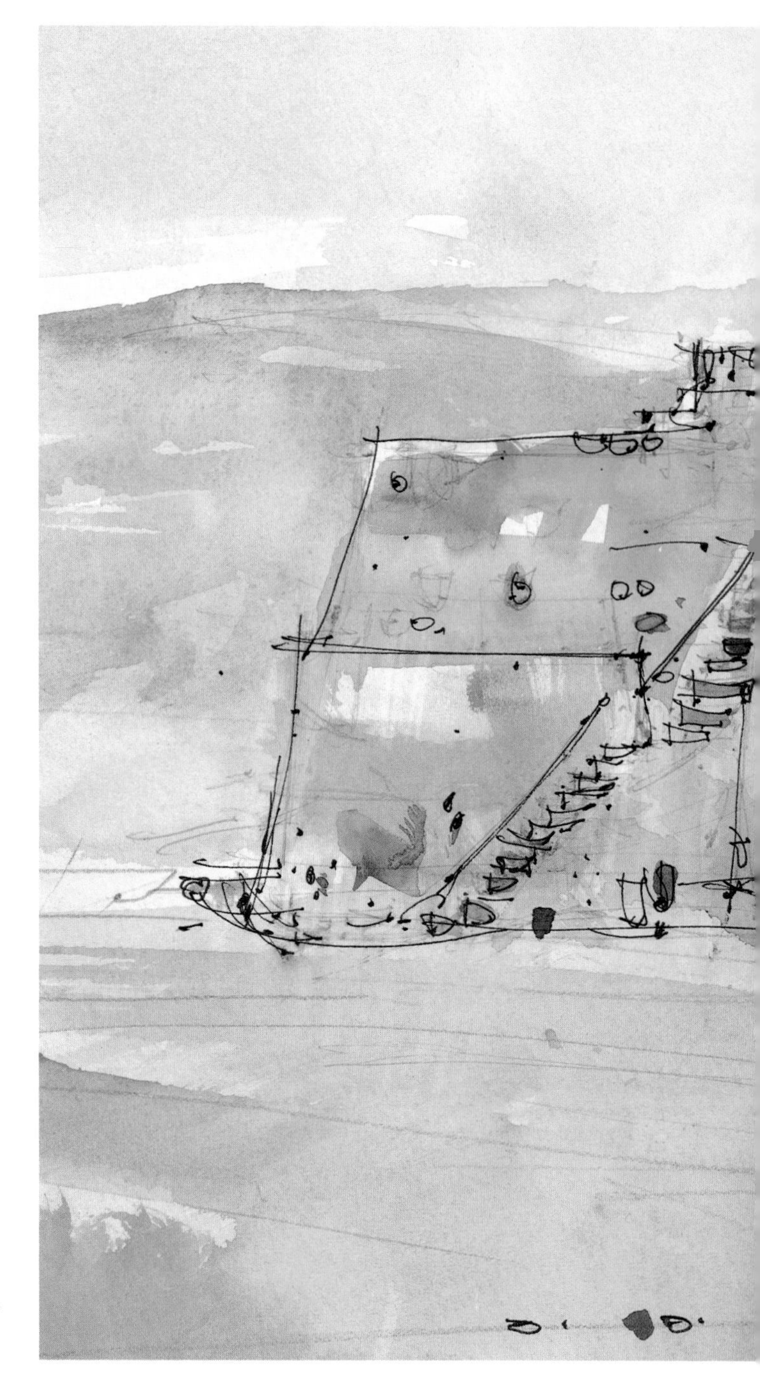

In this chapter I am going to introduce you to John's studio to give you an idea of his environment, and the various ways in which he compiles and uses reference material. John's work is highly individual, not to say unique. I had never seen anyone work in this way before, producing paintings which are free and pure.

You can't go to an art materials suppliers and buy many of the materials which John uses – such as the scruffy old brush which he prefers to use to one which is pristine and straight off the shelf! He either uses 90lb Bockingford or Arches paper, which he stretches onto sheets of hardboard. His big brushes are amazingly cheap one-inch and two-inch decorators' brushes which you could buy in the DIY shop – the kind normally used to paint railings or windows. He uses these primarily for his big, broad washes but also throughout the painting process. He ascertains that their crudity helps to produce interesting textures. He also uses a half inch sable which is incredibly scruffy and worn, to create interesting marks rather than a sharp-edged line. Much of his pencil work is done with a Papermate propelling pencil, which has a useful eraser in its end, never needs sharpening and produces a consistent line. However, he also uses 4-9Bs to add accents. Perhaps his most conventional brush is a no 2 or 3 round sable. He also uses an amazing collection of scruffy old paint boxes with half empty pans!

Other items which John works with include tissue paper, which he screws up and pats over his wet washes to provide texture, and masking tape instead of

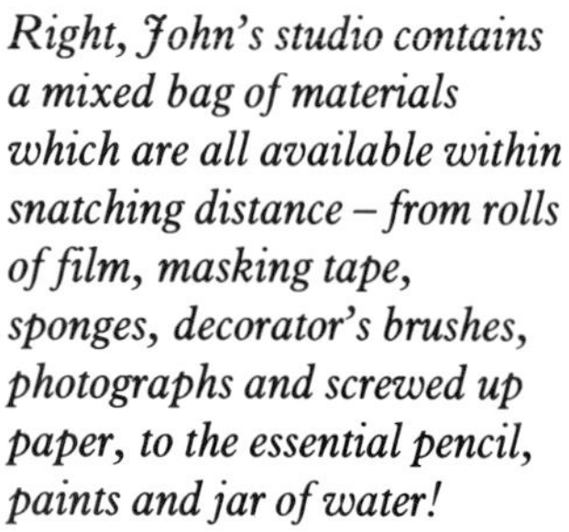

Right, John's studio contains a mixed bag of materials which are all available within snatching distance – from rolls of film, masking tape, sponges, decorator's brushes, photographs and screwed up paper, to the essential pencil, paints and jar of water!

Above, John has experimented here with the subject of landscape, incorporating a harbour into a mountainous scene. Pen and ink define the details of the features once the washes have dried and small touches of oil pastel are added to highlight important elements.

masking fluid for saving white areas of paper. He also uses a small sponge to wet his paper and later to produce further texture.

This amazing collection just goes to prove that it is not the materials alone which create the picture, in fact John admits that he abuses his materials to his own advantage! He uses them when ruined to break away from conventional strokes and obtain new effects.

It is worth looking around your studio for materials which you might not consider worthy of use. Sometimes the most unlikely tool will provide you with a special effect. The purchase of a small sponge, some tissue paper and some masking fluid will greatly increase your range of methods.

PRACTICE

○ In your studio keep a range of tissue paper, masking fluid, newspaper for masking, scissors, knives and used matchsticks for making marks.

○ Sponges can be used for lifting out colour or with paint for adding texture. If you apply one colour with a sponge to achieve a textured surface, wait until it is completely dry before adding a second to it.

○ Masking tape is useful for pressing onto dry watercolour if you want to put sparkle back into a heavy wash!

Left, John first designed the composition in pencil and masked out the shape of the bridge and foreground. He flooded blue across the sky diagonally. Once dry, he removed the masking fluid and added lighter washes and final details to the foreground.

Above, the masked area contrasts dramatically with the surrounding sky and land washes.

In both paintings, John uses a combination of loose washes and deliberate texturing techniques; spattering, wax resist, sponging, dry brush and drawing. All of these techniques can be practised in the studio, as long as you have the materials to hand!

This sky was achieved using a decorator's brush, flooding the wash on and allowing the colour to run its own course. Once dry, pencil work is added loosely to define the windmill, trees and illusion of foreground.

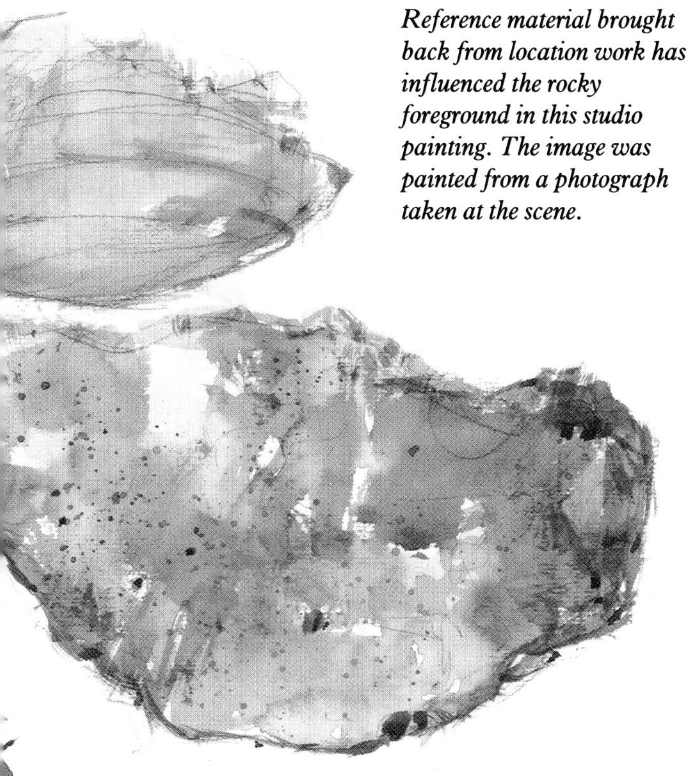

Reference material brought back from location work has influenced the rocky foreground in this studio painting. The image was painted from a photograph taken at the scene.

WORKING METHODS

To make the most of working in the studio you may wish to follow some of John's methods. For any given painting, he lays out a collection of photographs of the subject taken from different angles, material brought back from location visits and even examples of how other artists have tackled similar subjects. All this helps him to design the ultimate scene in his mind and is an important part of the preparation for a painting.

John uses two main methods to tackle his final paintings. He starts them all in the same way by stretching the paper – he may have half a dozen sheets ready-stretched on hardboard. From this point, the first method is to paint seemingly irrelevant, subtly coloured washes onto his paper. These may bear no relationship to the subject but provide him with inspiration for his initial pencil drawing on top, after the paper has dried. It also seems to make the finished painting appear more unified. His initial pencil drawing is done with a propelling pencil held in a unique way. The pencil hardly leaves the paper but

TECHNIQUES

John uses two main methods of working. He either works washes over pencil, or pencil over washes. When he makes initial pencil marks before adding the washes, he finds that he uses the brush as more of a drawing instrument, leaving areas of paper white to give a vibrancy to the illustration. In contrast, when he paints an overall wash before adding any pencil marks, he varies the strength of the washes but no areas of the paper will be left white.

Try to exercise your skills of representation by following one of John's techniques. Spend as little time as possible looking at your paper, and try guiding your hand and brush across the surface of the painting while keeping your eyes glued to the reference material before you.

wanders in a controlled but free manner, occasionally finishing with dots and then carrying on. It is an incredible process to watch, as John doesn't seem to look at his drawing at all, rather keeping his eyes on his reference or subject. He doesn't rough in the design lightly first, as many artists do, but allows the scene to evolve slowly from a central point. What is amazing is the confidence which gives the pencil line its own life. This is something which has been achieved by years of constant effort. His initial free washes contrast with more direct lines giving a unique quality of John's work.

FURTHER TECHNIQUES

The second method which John tends to follow is perhaps more usual, in that the initial drawing is first done on stretched white paper, then out come the decorators' brushes. When John is working in this way, he only wets parts of the paper, so he may apply

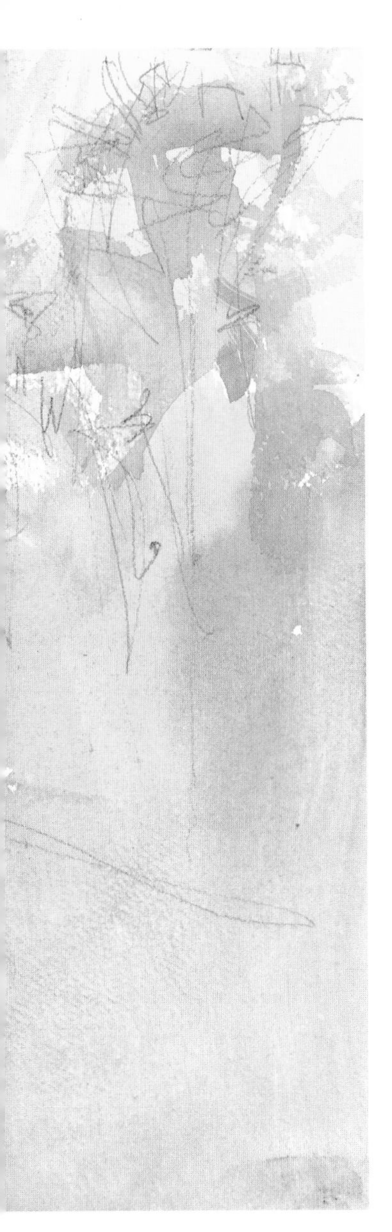

Left, to paint Warwick Castle, John laid down his washes prior to any pencil work, giving an overall tone to the painting before he began adding details.

Above, by contrast, in this painting John drew a pencil illustration before adding colour. This increases the vitality and spontaneity of the image and defines the buildings.

paint to both wet and dry patches. The colour is then added to these, with the artist showing little or no respect for working within the lines of his preliminary drawing. His primary concerns are to make sensitive marks and allow the paint a degree of freedom. John scumbles a lot and even uses his fingers to modify the washes and provide texture. The half inch scruffy sable is used for the more defined areas. These first washes are allowed to dry before he applies more pencil drawing, always unifying with the washes. The final drawing is done with the sable to provide emphasis. John is always conscious of keeping his colour schemes under control, often leaving it until the very end to add the touches of bright colour which pull the painting together. Even then they are always used with great discretion.

John may well be working on three paintings simultaneously, as he likes to stop half-way through to reconsider before proceeding. John frequently

PRACTICE

○ Spattering is a useful device for making texture on your painting. Once your work is completely dry, mask out all areas which you do not want to spatter. Fill the brush with paint, wipe off any surplus and then gently tap the ferrule with your finger to disperse it onto the paper. Ensure you direct your paint to the right area. Before you spatter a second colour, check that the first application is completely dry, otherwise the colours will run.

○ Instead of applying a flat wash across the surface of the paper, experiment with areas of wet and dry paper to add depth, highlights and texture to the image. You could even try painting with dry brush techniques directly onto the surface of the watercolour.

This painting utilises reference material; photographs and magazine illustrations. Collecting ideas together from such sources often stimulates John's imagination. Just because he is working in the studio, the artist does not have to limit his subject matter. This painting does not appear to be painted inside, and could have been created on site. John always attempts to retain freshness and simplicity in his work, wherever he creates it, but of course working in the studio enables him to be more adventurous! Primarily, this is a study in colour. Once the washes had been introduced into the sky, they were left alone. By building up the left-hand side of the painting with a little spattering, pen and ink drawing, pastel and sponging, balance and harmony are achieved. John is careful not to overdo the special effects, as it would be easy to imbalance the composition.

employs a mount as an extra aid in assessing the progress of the work.

There are many differences to be considered between working in the studio and working on location. When you are inside, you have far more control, and your materials are all easily to hand. John, incidentally, often has two or three brushes in his hand at the same time! You have plenty of flat table space on which to spread out your work, in direct contrast to working in an open field with your easel. This is particularly relevant to John's working method, for as well as his two or three brushes, he also

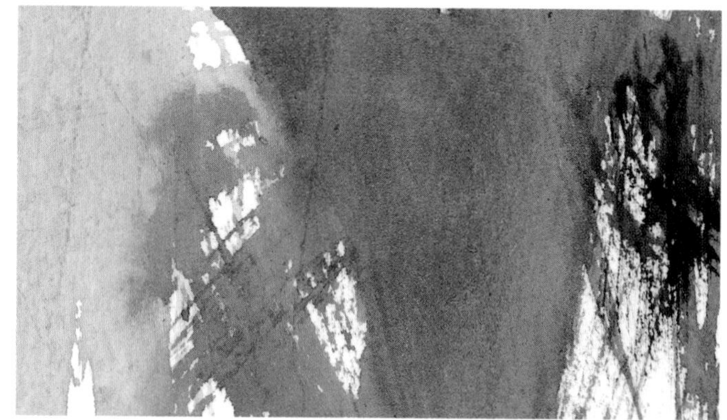

Combining watercolour washes with textures made from random spattering and pen line create unusual effects. They enhance the warm vision of the landscape, adding sparkle and vitality.

works from two or three paint boxes at the same time. However, don't get the impression that John's studio is like an operating theatre, it isn't. In fact it is almost chaotic – very informal and full of clutter! That is the way that he likes it, and I feel that this informality is reflected in the looseness of his paintings. Too much tidiness can be inhibiting and cause the work to tighten up. Having said that, though, discipline is also required – in other words it must be organised chaos! Each artist has his or her own personal way of working. You may find that you would benefit from extending your own range of methods.

Far left, pencil work and wash on extremely soft paper create a granular effect. John smudged some washes with his finger. When dry, he pressed masking tape to areas to create highlights.

Left, using a hog hair brush, John applied a wash with vertical pressure to create the appearance of flowing water.

Right, first John masked out fine lines to create stems, then washed in the colours for the foliage. Once dry, he removed the masking and with a fine sable painted the grasses. To add texture, he then scratched out highlights and added stippling.

A wintery, more conventional scene is again enhanced by the selective use of spattering and stippling. John also added pen lines and a dash of orange to counterbalance the colour composition.

Bits of heather and foliage, cones and seed heads are brought back from the landscape, along with tonal sketches done on the spot. These act as memory aids for John when painting this intense autumnal scene in the studio.

I asked John whether he painted sitting down or standing up, and he explained that he usually sits in his swivel chair to do the initial pencil drawings, but as the excitement grows and the free washes start to go on, his chair gets pushed back and he finishes off the painting standing up! He needs the room for plenty of free arm movement.

I have mentioned that, when working in the studio, John uses photographic references. I know that this is a controversial point, much frowned upon by staunch purists. To tackle the viewpoint head on, I would argue that, while of course there are dangers in using photographs, properly incorporated into the planning stages they can be a great help. The problem is that they are often misused. Anyone can copy a photograph but it takes experience and skill to produce a first class painting from one. The great disadvantage is that the shadows in them are often too strong and black, so have to be translated with plenty of transparent colour. If this is done with enough skill, it should be impossible to tell whether the painting has been done from photographs in the studio or out on site. Just one glance at John's paintings will completely support my argument! John never attempts to recreate the colour values which he sees in a photograph. In fact he makes a positive effort to avoid following the colours. If you find this difficult to do, try photostating your photograph so it becomes a black and white image.

John doesn't use any special lighting in his studio, relying mainly on an Anglepoise with a daylight bulb in it. However, in the summer the garden is brought into use as an extension to the studio, and his drawing board and materials are all moved outside. This helps to increase the freshness of the work.

Above, this painting was created on reflection of a seaside visit. The composition was developed in pencil and then heightened by washes. John has allowed the wash to flood and settle in pools where it accentuates the strength of the colour in contrast to the soft pencil gestures.

Left, working with the same techniques and tonal range, John has created a more rural landscape. The pencil work is more frenetic to enhance a sense of the leaves rustling in the trees.

PRACTICE

○ Take photographic reference on location to work from in the studio.

○ Only use photographs as a trigger for your memory – imagine them only as a window back into the real landscape.

○ Use imagination with your photographic image, otherwise your results will appear stilted and lifeless.

○ Force yourself to change the colour scheme you see in the photograph.

○ If you attempt to reproduce the colours seen on a print you will be in danger of painting a very flat, dull scene. If you find it difficult to avoid copying, take a photostat of the photograph and work from the black and white image which remains.

LANDSCAPE FEATURES

Having covered the more technical aspects of producing landscapes in watercolour, both on location and in the studio, I would like you to look, hopefully with a fresh eye, at some of the elements which will make up the content of your painting. Some may be new to you, as we have tried to look at the broad subject of watercolour landscape with an open mind. We have considered the question of light and atmosphere on the landscape and introduced subjects such as sporting activities, vehicles, buildings and people, but always as integral to the landscape, never as unrelated additions. In fact, the watchword for this whole section could well be integration. Although many of the features discussed could stand up on their own, in this case they are being used simply to enhance our landscapes to provide a different aspect of them. We also want to persuade you that the artist's job is to get away from the mundane and predictable and to produce paintings which are adventurous and stimulating.

John Palmer's work is an excellent example of this way of thinking. When he paints a tractor into a landscape scene, it is put in in exactly the same style as the rest of the landscape, and although authentic, leaves plenty to the imagination of the viewer. The same applies to his animals and buildings, in fact to all of the elements in his landscape. It's very important that you look at the pictures in this section analytically, rather than with casual admiration. There is an awful lot to learn here!

In this landscape you can see the full scope of the subject. Everything from rivers, boats, houses, trees, reflections in water, churches and bridges can be included to add interest. They are fully-integrated into the landscape, and their inclusion does not detract from the overall scene. You can be selective, of course, and do not have to include all of these features in one painting!

Light

The source of light in landscape is inevitably the sky, and its effects are infinitely variable and constantly on the move. Any landscape can change completely, depending on the weather effects above, be it clear sky, wind driven cumulus clouds casting their fast-moving shadows, or the rich gloom of an approaching storm. One of the first lessons to learn is to unify your sky with the landscape below and not treat them as two separate entities. One way of doing this is to provide visual links between them. You can also relate the general mood – for example the colour of water in a scene is strongly governed by the colour of the sky above it. With an overcast sky, the contrasts are less and values become closer.

Light can be manipulated by the artist to obtain unusual and exciting effects in a painting. For example, a patch of sunlit landscape against a dark, thundery sky can be intensely dramatic.

Light sources are analysed on a small pencil sketch on tinted cream paper before John embarks upon this brooding landscape scene below overcast skies.

TECHNIQUES

See how much variation you can achieve from a limited range of colours. This will discipline your work and also ensure that you achieve harmony of atmosphere, light and tone.

A limited range of colours will also create a balanced composition and emphasise the mood of the moment. Light and atmosphere run hand in hand!

The source of light across any landscape you paint is the sky. Be sensitive to its ever-changing nature. As clouds move and the rays of the sun become obscured or direct, so the light will change, and in turn so will the colours of the land below.

Above, by contrast, the oil pastel sketch on pale green tinted paper shows the landscape flooded with light.

Below, the final painting is muted in tone by the hazy, even quality of the light which suffuses it.

Unfortunately in nature these effects are fleeting and may last only for a few seconds. This is where the camera comes into its own as an aide-memoire. However, with experience and the use of creative tonal sketches, it is possible to start with a conventionally lit scene and then create these different effects in tone by rearranging the values. One of the greatest exponents of this was the late Rowland Hilder, who by careful and fastidious preparation before painting, could almost stage-light his subjects to give drama and interest. Another technique which he employed to great effect was the use of strong foreground shadow at the base of a painting, supposedly caused by an object outside the picture. This pushes the eye into the mid-distance where the strongly-lit centre of interest would be. These ideas can be fully appreciated by looking through Hilder's various books. Just as John creates his own colour schemes, Hilder would create his own lighting. It is impossible to try and change the lighting effects while you are actually painting. They must all be planned in your tonal sketch before you start.

In nature, one can often be faced with dull, overcast trees and houses, it is then up to you to improve the lighting by your practised knowledge and expertise. Remember though, that any creative lighting must be consistent. In other words, it must only come from one direction. Identify your source light and stick to it. A good exercise is to choose a subject, say a ruined

Simplicity is the key to the success of these works. The watercolour washes instil an atmosphere which is all-pervasive. The simplicity of design and reflective qualities of the landscape over the waterways show off the translucent nature of watercolour and its suitability for capturing light across landscape.

Left, this subject is dominated by the shape and angularity of the shadow itself. The light falls from the right casting cavernous shadows across half of the painting. Details are only suggested where bright light falls directly onto the building, intensifying the contrast between light and shade.

Right, a softer shadow falls across this gentle landscape. The horizontal nature of the shadows falling across the fields gives the illusion of depth and recession.

Bottom right, the shadows falling at dusk over this railway bridge create a cross-hatched pattern of bright light and deep shade.

abbey, and paint it first in morning mist and then later in strong afternoon light with lengthening shadows, creating an entirely different painting.

Many artists enjoy painting against the light, fascinated by the effects obtainable. Normally complex objects become simplified to shadowy shapes and scenes which could be discarded as too ordinary are given greater significance. This might be a good place to say a few words about shadows, which are basically an interruption of light. Once you understand them, shadows can be used to great advantage, and used properly will enhance a painting, helping to unify it and adding interest and excitement. Students often neglect shadows in their painting, therefore missing the opportunities they provide.

Cast shadows are important as they show up the profile of the surface they fall over and are especially

In these sketches shadows have been used in two ways. The first forms an archway around the subject, so that the eye is led through the image to the houses and landscape in the distance. In the second example, John uses the shadows to mould the shape of the buildings and introduce the foreground.

PRACTICE

When making preliminary sketches on location, mark in shadows and note the time of day. Return to the spot for an hour or two at the same time each day until the work is finished. Then the light and shade will remain constant – so long as the weather conditions do!
Do not over-complicate shadows in your paintings. Sometimes a simple stroke with the brush is all you need to suggest the direction of the light source.

These more developed paintings demonstrate how shadows can be used to dramatic effect.

Above, in this example, the shadows are apparent in sky, trees and land, creating contrast with the sun.

Right, the harsh diagonal shapes show an abstract pattern within which the shadows fall across the landscape.

valuable in creating snow scenes. Form shadows, creating for example the darker side of a building, again are often neglected by the inexperienced, yet they can provide great variety of tone in a painting.

From a watercolourist's point of view, what must be avoided are dull, flat, opaque shadows. They must always be transparent, allowing the original colour to show through. They should be added rapidly and with a sureness of touch. Once you have established where you are going to put the shadows, and what is causing them, they should be put in with a single sweep of the brush and then left alone. Sternly resist the temptation to touch them up or amend them once they are on the paper. Nothing looks worse than an overworked shadow! Aim for luminosity, warmth and speed of application. My own colour preference for shadows is a mixture of ultramarine and light red. Half-way between the two gives you a warm mauve grey. Too thick and it will cover up the underlying colours, too weak and you will be tempted to put on that fatal second coat. For snow scenes, you need a little more blue.

Don't neglect bounced light either. For example, the colour of the ground will bounce into the shadowed area of the building. Finally, at the point where the shadow on a building touches the lit side, it

always appears to be darker. This is called plane change accent. From this point the shadow should always begin to lighten.

One lighting effect which always seems to fascinate beginners is the single shaft through a cloud. Everyone wants to know how it can be obtained. Most experienced painters I know are inclined to use an ink eraser when the painting is dry to create the effect. Personally I think it can easily be overdone and produce a cliché. Watercolour is a wonderful medium for creating light effects, and nothing is fresher than using the white paper for highlights. The luminosity of watercolour paint is greater than any other medium and must be preserved at all costs. Edward Wesson felt that watercolour had a unique quality, the key being the paper itself. The process of painting should disturb the surface of the paper as little as possible. Pushing the paint around and manipulating it will only destroy its magic. If you spend too much time painting over one area of the paper, or scratch out, mask or erase too much paint, the surface will be destroyed forever.

The vigorous, scudding clouds enliven the breeze-filled sky and denote the ever-changing nature of the scene. In contrast, the land appears still and solid, a fact reinforced by the position of the boat and its mast.

PRACTICE

○ Always be on the look out for light effects; the appearance of a rainbow, a sudden storm obscuring three quarters of the landscape or dramatic cloud formations. When cloud shadows hit the landscape, the colours change and shafts of light created can highlight a single object or feature. Make a mental note so that you can introduce these effects into your work. It is sometimes worth concluding a painting with some dashes of vivid colour applied in a different medium to pick out features. Oil pastel or coloured pencil are useful supplementary media to have to hand.

Left, skies are not always blue! At different moments of the day in different climates, the sky might appear as anything from pale ochre to peach. In this instance a soft blend of grey and pale ochre creates a neutral sky which complements the ephemeral landscape beneath.

Above, the blue sky contrasts with low-lying grey clouds creating a busy and tempestuous skyscape.

Above, a winter scene is enhanced by a diluted pale pink counterbalanced by the cool greys leading to the foreground creating a flat skyscape.

Right, a combination of quite unexpected colours create this autumnal sky. John uses pale ochre, through cool grey graduating towards pale lemon. In all of these sky scenes, John has made use of very definite brushstrokes, often applying the paint in broad sweeps.

Above, dusk settling over a summer's day is enhanced by the orange glow of the sky warming the land mass lying beneath.

Above, a cool spring day is captured by the mixture of blue paint and areas left white in the sky. This creates a fresh, breezy mood across the woodland.

Atmosphere

This leads us on to that indefinable subject: atmosphere. Without it painting is bland, and yet it is almost impossible to describe. It cannot be manufactured, but has to be felt within if there is to be any chance of it being interpreted through your brush. It is like listening to a piece of music being played by two different pianists. Both may technically be correct, but while one will fail to touch your emotions, the other will move you to tears.

The use of colour is an important factor when portraying atmosphere. Warm and rich or cool and subtle, all create their own atmosphere. A lively

The lack of definition in these compositions enhances the atmospheric qualities of the scenes. John makes full use of the translucency of watercolour.

Below, a winter evening is painted in monochrome, its composition reminiscent of Japanese watercolours.

Right, the heat haze is captured in a variegated wash, with only the head being given any definition.

fairground atmosphere can be obtained by a kaleidoscope of colour. Single spots of bright colour in an otherwise subdued painting can create excitement. But beware, too much colour will destroy on impact. Another way to achieve this atmosphere is to concentrate colour and impact in one part of the picture, then fade off the colour and details as you move away from it. Also remember to leave periods of silence in your painting, allowing the viewer's mind to concentrate entirely on the main object of interest.

Of course the weather will change with the seasons, and painting from the same location all year round can give immense satisfaction. Each season has its own charm. In the spring, although you are beginning to see new leaves, you can still perceive the basic network of branches. This can be a beautiful combination, but

Left, John has created a subdued landscape in early winter, the mist rising from the fields. This is a simple design. The eye is allowed periods of silence where it may rest and absorb the atmosphere of the scene, before moving around the image and concentrating on the details it then encounters. Sometimes it is worth leaving free space within the composition – don't feel that your landscape has to be crowded with detail. Often atmosphere and harmony are best-evoked through simplicity of design – enjoy creating it!

Top, a diluted wash of raw sienna has been used to give tonal depth and warmth to this sketch. The counterchange of blue intensifies the richness of the original colour.

Above, by contrast, the brightness of this lemon yellow and ochre wash draws the abstract landscape forwards on the paper, making the image more immediate and startling than in the previous example.

remember that the greens are still delicate, yellowy-green and fresh. As we move towards summer, the greens become warmer and richer and the shadows stronger. In autumn be careful not to overdo the rich colours. It is easy to make the whole painting too bright. Better to restrict the real brightness to small areas. And don't fall into the trap of making the scene too cold in winter. Try to introduce areas of warm brown colour to contrast and act as a foil to the cold blues and greys.

As watercolourists, I have always felt that we are lucky, as our medium with its speed allows us to capture the fast-moving effects of light and shade.

TECHNIQUES

Try to do a complete painting on a stretched, damp piece of paper. Mark out the areas which you would like to apply different colours to very lightly in pencil. Use complementary colours to enhance the tonal qualities of the watercolour. Apply the areas of colour with a wide brush, tilting the paper to a slight angle while you work, to encourage the watercolour to drift. Once dry, you will have a soft, atmospheric background onto which you can add the details of your landscape scene. This technique will free you to really use your imaginative skills, as the atmosphere evoked may now be enhanced by any features introduced.

Be aware of the warm and cool colours in your palette and work across a tonal range which complements the season you are painting. Do not overdo the warm colours in autumn. If you do your painting may appear gaudy. In winter scenes a touch of warm colour will add vitality to the scene without affecting the mood of the scene.

A purely imaginative landscape, not taking anything into consideration other than John's great pleasure in using the watercolour medium.

Water

An inseparable aspect of landscape painting is water in all its many guises. Maybe I am prejudiced, but over half of my own paintings include water in some form or another and John too loves to portray this subject. We both feel that there is no better medium for portraying water in all its translucency than watercolour itself. One of the earliest mistakes we all make is to try too hard and too earnestly to capture this elusive element. We have to learn through bitter experience to handle it delicately, lightly and with an enormous economy of stroke. In the beginning we overfuss it, putting in too many ripples, tipping it up as it goes around bends, believing somehow that the more fiddling we do, the better it will look. The answer, however, is to learn merely to symbolise water. Simplicity and speed are the keynotes. Personally, I always paint in the rest of the picture first, leaving the water until the end, rather like someone saving the cherry on top of the cake until the last delicious mouthful! To me it is certainly the most exciting element of all to portray, whether it is a peaceful pond or a raging rapid. I decide which technique to use, and almost 'psych' myself up to let fly as rapidly as possible!

To paint water with confidence, you need to understand its characteristics. Knowledge of all its forms, whether calm or turbulent, will enable you to paint with authority and confidence. Before talking about these various forms, perhaps we should consider some of the faults we have to overcome. The most common is the tendency to make rivers flow uphill in the distance, or tip over as they go around bends. This is inevitably due to lack of observation. When you see an area of river in front of you, try to think of it merely as a shape to be reproduced on paper. If this is done accurately there will be no more trouble, but so many painters paint what they think they see, not what they

There is no medium quite like watercolour for capturing the effects of water in a landscape! In this case, John has exploited the medium in a saturated tonal study of a mist-filled sky above a lake. The composition is unified by the close tonal relationships and then counterpointed by a dash of red and blue.

actually see. Avoid too, meaningless ripples, and concentrate on reflections in calm water and capturing movement in rapids. Give rivers plenty of perspective, don't make them parallel as they run into the distance. It is almost impossible to over-exaggerate the width of a river in the foreground or its taper as it moves into the distance. Remember, overfussing must be avoided at all costs. It will not enhance the work.

First let us consider calm water such as slow-moving rivers and ponds. Perhaps the first thing to understand is that water, having no colour of its own, reflects everything around it. For instance, the sky above will inevitably affect the colour of the water below, whether it be a stormy purple, a clear blue or the dramatic reflections of a sunset.

Next come the objects adjacent to the water, the tree trunks, posts or rocks. These too will appear upside down, as softened mirror images. Regarding these factors, try to study reflections as often as possible. It doesn't matter if you haven't got your paints with you,

Below left, John denotes the still, mirror-like qualities of the water, showing the way in which it reflects surrounding buildings and trees.

Right, the rushing waterfall is depicted by vertical brush marks which contrast with a horizontal skyline and calm pool of water settled beneath.

practise really looking and carrying the information back to your studio in your memory for future reference. In my own painting I like to indicate a pale streak of disturbed water but one could say that this is personal idiosyncrasy.

Moving on to disturbed water such as large lakes or estuaries, the distant reflections disappear and only those in the immediate foreground, such as posts, will appear. These should be indicated simply with a wiggle. Background hills, however, will still affect the colour of the water below. Now to fast-moving water, the most exciting of all to paint. Here the directional strokes of the brush are most important. In fact the faster the river, the faster the stroke. Also, here you can leave almost 50% of the paper untouched to indicate foam. Observation beforehand is vitally important. Looking at the water for a few minutes will show you the repeated pattern of movement. With this knowledge firmly in your head, paint as economically and rapidly as possible. It also helps to break up the water with rocks, which will add counterchange and

PRACTICE

○ Practice masking out a single very fine line right across an area of water to create reflections. Make the bottom edge straight, the top slightly broken, dividing the area above and below the waterline. Wash colour over the entire area and allow it to dry. Remove the masking fluid and the area around the highlight will be more intense in colour than across the rest of the wash. From this point you will be able to practise creating an image above the line and its reflection below.

○ In much the same way as when painting skies or shadows, water can often be denoted by the simplest of brushmarks on the paper. Gestural strokes can create the most effective water masses. Flooding the paper with water and then dropping colours into it will allow watercolour to drift and blur, creating the illusion of pools of water.

Below, the tonal sketch shows the patterns of water and land, marking in the repetitions and movement across the composition.

Left, the stark angularity of the cliffs contrasts with the fluid movement of the sea below.

Above, the illusion of water is created through a pattern of overlapping washes.

Right, a combination of washes and textural effects gives the impression of reflected reeds in a pond.

Above, estuary at dusk giving glimpses of a village, hills and river bank. A subtle variegated wash has been applied across the paper to suggest the flow of water, reinforced by the later addition of a sailing boat.

Right, using a wider brush, John has overlaid broad washes with brush work to define the water, lakeside and distant mountains.

Above, here John has used slightly rougher paper and masking fluid. The background washes were applied loosely and the colour was allowed to flow down the paper to give the impression of water. The building, by contrast, is blocked in almost impasto fashion.

PRACTICE

○ Water comes in many forms in a landscape so use it imaginatively! From rushing streams to sedate lakes, wide open estuaries to winding rivers incorporate them to add excitement.

○ Use water to create unusual compositions as John has, for example, cascading over a rock face into the pool below.

○ Water is made up of the colours surrounding it, reflecting off its surface; greens of the land, blues of the sky.

tonal excitement. The faster you paint your brushstrokes, the more dynamic the effect will be. Quick marks or overlaying washes will enhance the fast movement of the water.

Returning for a moment to estuaries – a beautiful subject for landscape, the different and elegant shapes created by the water at low tide providing a study of their own as well as a lovely background for any boats, birds or human figures you want to introduce. These paintings are always popular – and sell very well too!

Do not neglect cloud shadows on large stretches of water. They are invaluable in helping to create interest in what could otherwise be a rather plain surface. Two more aspects of water which can be exploited are flooded fields and puddles. In the first you will get fascinating patterns provided by the reflections of gates, posts and fences, and the second will add sparkle and interest to country lanes or, equally effectively, to city pavements.

Trees

Trees are a very important part of landscape but must be properly integrated into your painting. In terms of picture design, they are vital elements. In an otherwise horizontal composition, a foreground tree will provide the one vertical element which will prevent monotony and hold the picture together, linking the foreground with the background, the sky with the land, in fact unifying the whole painting. Trees are good devices for indicating depth and recession, you can achieve this by painting one strong foreground tree and then reducing the rest in tone and size as you move towards the background. Regarding composition, there are, as always, hazards to avoid. Never paint two trees of exactly the same size and weight on either side of a picture. Always make sure one tree dominates. Avoid, too, boring repetition of trees without variation, in other words change the angles, widths and general shapes throughout the picture. Another way to create unity is to use a tree shape to echo a cloud on the opposite side of the painting.

Let us consider trees now in terms of counterchange. They can be used to emphasise the importance of features such as a white house or sail, by providing a dark shape behind it, which immediately creates interest. Remember too, in a single tree, to paint it light against a dark background, then, as it reaches the sky, change it to dark against light.

A combination of watercolour and line work create an intense and unusual composition. The trees close into a copse, almost as if an internalised landscape. A strong mix of ultramarine alongside ochres and a dash of orange enhance the scene.

Above, the trees in this painting have been used to enhance the composition and demonstrate their wide scope as design tools. Not only do they frame the distant fields and hills, but they also lead the eye through the painting from the foreground to the middle distance, where they become more abstracted forms.

Left, in this sketch the stark winter trees are the only feature in an otherwise empty landscape. The pale ochre wash of the sky and background contrasts with the areas of the trunks left white, emphasising the simplicity of their design.

The various seasons can be indicated by the use of colour in your trees. Autumn is best portrayed by russet shades in the foreground and mauves in the background, which will add depth. Winter scenes need plenty of blue greys and umbers, while in springtime scenes, fresh yellowy-greens will predominate. In the summer the greens are warmer and richer with more ochre in them. As well as indicating seasons, trees can also symbolise the location of a scene. Pines and palm trees tell completely different stories.

The use of tree shadows too can be of great importance in a painting. The shadow of a foreground tree can be used to form a rich, dark base for a painting. This device was taken a stage further and used to great effect by Rowland Hilder. He would add shadow right across the base of his scene, apparently caused by a tree just outside the painting, increasing the dramatic impact of a well-lit tree or building in the middle ground. In winter, foreground trees provide an ideal opportunity for calligraphy as a foil for flat areas elsewhere in the painting.

Moving back into distant woodlands, remember

Above, the sketch is simplified into three colours, pale grey/blue, ultramarine blue and a touch of ochre. The tree is reduced to the two blue tones and painted in a series of cross-hatched lines with a fine sable to create texture.

that trees in groups lose their identity and become a single, flat mass or bars of colour, but a mass which must be varied in colour, again to avoid monotony. Returning to foreground trees, a mark of the amateur is to paint them in a single boring colour, usually brown. The artist should instead take the opportunity of using plenty of varied colour and texture, perhaps cooler at the top and warmer towards the base. You may not actually see this variation of colour in reality, but remember that one of your roles as an artist is to be an entertainer. Having mentioned the base, it is important too that the tree should really grow out of the ground rather than appear to be perched on top of it in a precarious fashion.

Optically speaking, do not let limbs leave the trunk opposite one another, but stagger them. Limbs, trunks, and branches should be composed of straight lines, not curves. They gradually decrease in width as

PRACTICE

○ To create texture in your foliage and trees, practise mixing media. A little touch of oil pastel or wax crayon can give the illusion of leaves and undergrowth.

○ Sponging two or three colours over an area can create effective foliage, as can spattering colours. Remember to allow one colour to dry when attempting these techniques.

○ Don't be misguided into believing that trees are always brown. The trunks are often a blend of greys and greens, much like the branches and leaves.

○ If your trees appear flat, make sure that the branches protrude at different angles and include extra tonal variation.

Three very different approaches to painting trees can be seen on these pages. Left, exotic palms in a tropical setting are accentuated by feathered brushstrokes. Right, allowing ink to run and spread across the branches of a beech tree enhances the weight of the foliage. Far right, in contrast, outlined shapes drawn with a brush emphasise the angularity of plane trees.

Different seasons can easily be suggested by the inclusion of trees.

Above, only the evergreens survive in this harsh winter landscape.

Below, the autumnal woodland is imbued with warm oranges and rich ochres, overlaid with brush work to suggest the shape of leaves, branches and trunks.

Below, a summer landscape is enhanced by the inclusion of trees whose shadows dominate the scene. They throw dappled light across the composition, depicted here by areas left white. Trees do not have to be painted with brown trunks! Here it is enough to suggest their presence through the application of various green tones and a touch of blue to enhance their forms.

they go from trunks to twigs.

Foreground features such as hedges, bushes and textures should be handled with care and discretion to avoid overworking them. They can often be the downfall of an otherwise successful painting. Both John and I find that the faster you do them, the better they are. Here too, that word monotony creeps in again, and can only be avoided by using plenty of varied colour and texture, even if you cannot actually see it in the subject before you.

Bushes, like trees, can be used to counterchange objects next to them, such as fences or walls, but again, make sure that the sizes are varied and do not dot them around your painting indiscriminately. Try to integrate them into groups to ensure unity.

Hedges and fences can be used as positive design tools to take the viewer's eye to wherever the artist wants it to go, which is usually the main point of interest. They should never be parallel but, like roads, should taper strongly as they recede into the distance.

TECHNIQUES

Don't try and create too much detail in distant trees. Think of them as a series of shadowy shapes rather than individual trees. A simple way to create this effect is to lay a broken wash on the horizon, allow it to dry and then brush in a series of marks denoting the direction that the shadows take. Add one or two lines for the trunks of the trees to connect the shapes with the land beneath them.

Although colours in the foreground of a painting tend to be more intense than those in the mid-distance or background, do not make the contrast between such features as foreground hedges and trees in the distance too great. You could easily ruin a painting by overworking close features, dividing the painting too harshly.

Roads and Paths

Top, despite the fact that the path leads directly through the middle of the painting, the support of the trees and distant houses make for an interesting and mysterious composition.

Above left, the two gateposts in shadow lead the eye through the painting, between the trees which frame the scene.
Above right, the river acts as a natural pathway.

Here the centre of interest lies in the middle distance. The path begins in the bottom right hand corner of the painting and sweeps the eye across the empty foreground to the clump of trees lying directly diagonal to its point of departure, in the top right hand corner. From this point, John has cleverly created a line of buildings which lead the eye back across the horizon to rest at the point from which it originally entered the painting!

When indicating roads and paths there are, as always, some pitfalls to be avoided. For example, the sides of roads should never be parallel – this always looks unconvincing and shows a lack of knowledge of common perspective. As with rivers, the width of the road should greatly diminish as it recedes into the distance. In fact, it is almost impossible to over-exaggerate its width in the foreground. As a road curves and twists, it becomes much narrower. Avoid, too, the temptation to 'tip the road up' to show its width as it changes direction.

From a design standpoint, a road should never be straight. Within reason, the longer the route, the longer you will be able to keep the eye of your viewer within the picture, as with rivers. You may achieve this by curving the road before it gets to the edge of the painting or by 'blocking' it – putting something over it, such as a tree.

One sees so many paintings of flat, grey roads! Try to introduce plenty of gradation of both colour and tone, from palest blues through mauves and pinks to rich browns and terracottas. You may protest that you can't actually see these colours, but have faith, they will enhance your picture and avoid the artist's greatest enemy: monotony. A path also provides opportunities to introduce the complementary colours into a picture, for example, light red in a predominantly green woodland scene. This would look particularly exciting if mauve and transparent shadows of the trees across the path were introduced.

Try to confine texture to the absolute foreground, taken too far back it will destroy the illusion of distance. Shadows are another useful adjunct across roads and paths and should not be neglected, particularly in the foreground, where they can be used to show up the contour of the road and possible ruts.

Roads can be a useful design device for leading one's eye through a picture to the main object of interest, but once there, you must not disappoint your viewers. Give them something worthwhile to look at, no matter how small it is in relation to the whole picture. Some of the most compelling distant features are manmade objects, whether they comprise a house, boat, church or even a simple gate.

Buildings

Don't bypass buildings in landscapes in favour of rivers and trees, simply because it takes more effort and concentration to suggest them authentically! The extra work and concentration is infinitely worthwhile, as they will make your landscapes become more diverse and therefore more interesting.

When you are depicting buildings in the distance, the temptation to put in detail must be sternly resisted at all times. In fact, often the distant object or figure can be reduced to a simple silhouette. It is the actual profile which identifies it that must be drawn carefully and in proportion. Once this is achieved, the absolute minimum of strokes should be used for completion. You can forget about window frames or the details of each brick in a wall at half a mile. The corner of a one brush is quite sufficient to show such features at that distance. Don't even contemplate drawing tiles on a roof. What is important, however, if you really want to attract your viewer's attention, is counterchange.

Light objects may be positioned against a darker background, and vice versa. This, of course, also applies to figures. The counterchange, however, must be discreet. Remember we are talking about distance, so the contrast must be played down. Really dramatic contrasts should be saved for the foreground.

See distant buildings or townscapes as an overall pattern of blocks. This will help you to link the buildings to each other in size and colour.

Left, this unusual tonal study shows the breakdown of buildings into abstract blocks. The use of warm tones against white blocks is suggestive of a town rising up out of the desert. Experimenting with design elements in this way will help you understand their values more fully.

An ancient city on the horizon can add a further dimension to landscape painting. The buildings may enhance the contours of the land and skylines and add interest to your composition while also creating a frame around it.

The landscape in this scene exists in the distance, the buildings and harbour dominating the foreground. The painting still rests within the landscape tradition, however, as nature frames the entire scene.

Our most important task is to convey character, whether it be a modern barn or a thatched cottage. This will indicate the period and location of your painting, wherever you are. For instance, a colourful cafe exterior with its bright awnings and crowded tables will immediately suggest continental Europe rather than the UK, whereas the quiet atmosphere of a cathedral is purely English. American scenery and architecture too, has a quality of its own, apart from the city skyline, most of the small towns have wooden buildings which are quite unique. US church architecture too is quite different to the European, probably due to the materials used. In the Greek Islands, the buildings have a flavour all of their own, with their terracotta roofs, white walls, and brightly coloured shutters. The angles of the roofs, incidentally, are usually much shallower than those in colder climates. Here, too cypress trees can be useful to counterchange against white walls!

Figures, of course, will always give scale to buildings. Make sure you paint them loosely and in the same style, keeping them in groups rather than dotting them about indiscriminately. Train your eyes to take in the profile of a group of buildings. This is the quickest way to establish character and unity.

Make sure your buildings are an integral part of the landscape which they inhabit. Unfortunately, it is all too easy to tighten your style as soon as you tackle them. You will often see paintings in which buildings could well have been added by a different artist altogether as the style is so different.

In the UK some of the loveliest ancestral homes were designed and built to blend with and complement the landscape, so the least you can do is reproduce them in your paintings. Always connect buildings with the landscape. Shadows and trees are very useful in this respect, as they can be used to interlock the two elements.

Left, these ancient monuments are relics from a past time, still standing within this contemporary landscape.

Right, by contrast, in this painting John has chosen to depict cooling towers of the modern age – perhaps a structure many artists would choose to ignore in their landscapes, even though they exist!

TECHNIQUES

When painting buildings into a landscape don't attempt to depict every window, brick or roof tile. More gestural strokes will give the impression of the structures without making them dominate the scene.

Concentrate your eye on the profile of a group of buildings. It will make them easier to depict.

Speaking of shadows, great dramatic effect can be brought into your landscapes by portraying buildings almost as shadows on the skyline, while retaining their shape and character. Another way to integrate buildings and landscape is by unifying colour.

Buildings in landscapes need not only be old and traditional. Look at the exciting shapes created by modern technology in the form of cooling towers, radio masts and pylons. John maintains that these are the modern equivalents of windmills and must not be ignored. Bridges too come into the scope of buildings, as do viaducts and railway stations. All these offer themselves as natural foils to trees and hills.

One last word of warning. Don't get so carried away with your portrayal of buildings that you forget the basic rules, and place them bang in the centre of your painting! Try to place them in an interesting context and one which is pleasing to the eye. Have a good look at John's work and see how he has managed to combine the freedom of line with a mere suggestion of detail – with authenticity.

The buildings in these three paintings have become wholly integrated into the surrounding landscape.

Above left, although the buildings dominate the skyline, the overall wash unites the illustration. The forms of the buildings are first drawn in pencil, then loose shapes are washed over them, following the line of the buildings. The green of the landscape is suggested fleetingly, but seems to flow back into the fabric of the buildings.

Bottom left, in contrast, the buildings here form a dramatic frame for the landscape beyond.

Right, here the landscape and buildings are so completely integrated that you cannot distinguish land mass from manmade structures. They are unified by the dramatic triangles of sky and sea which surround them.

Movement

No landscape should be completely static. There is often movement in a scene, whether farmers inspecting their land, cricketers playing a match, animals grazing or cars driving up country lanes. The movement they create will add life and vitality to your landscape. If your painting lacks a centre of interest and you want to add movement, use your imagination to create an interesting narrative and enliven the scene. There are many ways to do so!

FIGURES

Nothing can make or mar a picture so much as the addition of figures. Artists lacking in confidence will either leave them out altogether or put them in with too much detail, in a completely different style. It is important though that figures enhance the painting. Generally, the less detail the better, but it is the proportions that are crucial – keep heads small and figures tall and usually leave out the feet!

If you are drawing groups of people, take care not to space them out equally. Like trees in a wood they can easily lose their individuality and become blocks. Counterchange light figures against dark backgrounds or dark figures against light backgrounds. Their shadows will help to anchor them and also indicate the light source.

The difficulty most of us have is to get the scale right in different parts of the picture. One idea is to draw the figures on tracing paper first and move them around until you are happy with their positioning.

Figures can also help denote season and weather conditions – you can indicate wind by having figures leaning into it, perhaps holding onto their hats. Get plenty of colour and movement into your figures and when you are painting groups or couples make them into a unit, rather than putting light between them.

More often than not figures will become the main point of interest in a landscape scene, however small or distant they are. Ensure that they are evoking the atmosphere you are trying to convey – be it that of a

Incorporating features such as these cricketers not only adds narrative interest to your scene, but also provides movement which brings the painting to life. By overlapping the washes a sense of movement is reiterated in the actual flow of paint.

Above, the bob-sleigh speeds down hill, suggesting high latitudes. John overlays washes to integrate the footballer into the landscape. The golfers are postioned to emphasise the artist's high perspective.

Left, the sailing boat suggests extreme speed and blustery conditions, emphasised by the use of highlights. The weather conditions and marine activity contrast with the solid and undulating landscape resting against the horizon.

busy harvesting scene on a farm, a leisurely summer afternoon stroll through the meadows, or the harsh force of nature against a sole figure battling against the elements to find shelter.

SPORTING SCENES

The field of sport offers whole new opportunities for painting landscape with a difference, each sport becoming part of the landscape in its own particular way. However, each sport also presents you with its own particular challenge of incorporating the activity in a way which enhances the landscape scene. Not an easy task, it calls for great design skill and a knowledge of the activity. The sportsman involved will be your greatest critic and will instantly be aware of a lack of initial research on your part. Conversely, if you succeed, you will find enormous appreciation among sportsmen and a willingness to dig deep into their pockets for the chance to buy your work. Specialising in this field, one can soon build up a reputation among the sporting fraternity and regular commissions might well come your way!

Golf lends itself particularly well to this form of landscape painting, set as it inevitably is among attractive scenery. The smooth greens, the rough and the sand, present opportunities for combining your techniques to show up their various colours and textures. Imagine, too, the 18th hole with the club house in the background, tiny figures and your choice of sky to indicate weather conditions. Surely this is a marvellous chance to use your artistry. As golf is played in all weathers, so a particular scene will never be the same two days running. It is worth pausing here for a moment to consider going into print on a particularly successful painting. Generations of golfers will continue to purchase a good picture of their favourite hole, to display in their homes.

Sailing is another attractive prospect, and here we are looking at waterscapes. There are wonderful moments to capture as people prepare their boats for a race. Scenes can be colourful with the flash of yellow life jackets and the bright colours of the sails. Again, technical bloomers must be avoided at all cost once the sailing is under way. There is the sparkle of water and the various angles of the boats as they jockey for position, rounding the buoys, which present another point of colour, not forgetting, of course, the vivid colours of the spinnakers.

There are many areas where boats form a natural part of the landscape. A typical example of this is Norfolk, England, where the flat land presents the artist with enormous skies, what I think of as Seago country. One of the delights of the area until a few years ago was the sight of boat sails apparently moving across green fields. It still happens, of course, but not as often as it used to. Design-wise it is a wonderful opportunity to counterchange a white sail against a dark tree, providing a lovely, natural focal point.

So many fine paintings have been, and will be, produced of these huge, windswept skies, low horizons and the flash of a white sail. Most estuary scenes at low tide cry out for a stranded dinghy to provide a centre of interest. They also provide the opportunity to add a touch of different colour. Never, however, give in to the temptation to include every detail, you will only over-complicate the image.

Cricket provides a more placid and leisurely atmosphere. The village green, for example, can provide a beautiful setting with its club house and tea tent. The challenge here may be avoiding an erratic composition because of the widely scattered players. You you may choose instead to concentrate on a particular player as he pads up.

Bowling greens can also be excellent subjects. Again, you have the architectural challenge of the club house, while the players themselves will probably be

Above, animals not only add a sense of movement to the landscape, they can also create an all-pervasive and intense stillness.

Left, the horse appears to rise up out of the undergrowth. The colour scheme is intentionally muted to harmonise the very fabric of the landscape with the horse and its rider.

Right, a simple detail of seagulls soaring above a beach. The sand is evoked by the judicious use of spattering.

TECHNIQUES

To integrate figures fully into the landscape always work in the same style right across the picture – regardless of the particular elements you are painting. Detail will give character. Sometimes a bright touch of colour will add vitality – a speck of red on a hat, a hint of yellow on a mast or stripes across a footballer's shirt.

Use sporting scenes to enhance a landscape, such as boats floating on the Norfolk Broads, as if by magic.

Below, the deer counterbalance against the trees and foliage and add narrative interest to this otherwise quite conventional scene. The simple image of horses and cart are enhanced by the use of shadow which roots them into the landscape.

Right, this image shows, perhaps more than any other, how sporting features may be added to a landscape scene to give interest but not detract from the country setting.

the main attraction, with their pristine uniforms and earnest expressions.

In complete contrast, the racing scene is one of constant excitement and movement, the ring with glossy horses and brightly-coloured silks of the jockeys contrasting with the more somberly clad owners. Movement is all here. Do not be be afraid of portraying horses, they can be indicated in a free and loose way, thus avoiding the need for anatomical accuracy. Your main task is to convey the excitement and colour – the white buildings and rails are an excellent foil to all this. While we are on the topic of horses, hunting gives an excellent opportunity for you to combine the movement and colour of the hunt with beautiful scenery – what more could you wish for?

Finally to fishing. This is possibly the ideal way of integrating sport with landscape painting. A single fly

fisherman standing in the rushing river, counterchanged against the dark trees, always makes an arresting subject and focal point. The rows of umbrellas along a bank during a fishing competition, under the threatening skies, make another good subject and evoke a completely different atmosphere. And the tackle and catch create an interesting composition for a still-life in a landscape.

ANIMALS

Of course animals are often an integral part of the landscape, and offer untold possibilities for the painter. There is no getting away from the fact that the only way to become competent in indicating animals in landscape in a casual yet authentic way is to spend time sketching them. When you are able to show a totally believable sheep or a cow by what appears to be a mere smudge, you can be sure that you have spent countless hours drawing them beforehand.

All animals have certain characteristics which must show through. For instance, deer are always delicate and alert to danger, while cockerels are real posers as they strut about the farmyard. Dogs spend much time with their noses to the ground, as do cows, who are usually eating, while cats are often in repose.

It is unwise, unless you are very experienced, to just 'make up' an animal to complete a painting. Either paint it on the spot, or use a good photographic reference to ensure its authenticity. And, as with any other feature, make sure that it is an integral part of the landscape, not just added as an afterthought. Animals are an effective feature to "place" your scene within a specific context. Of course you will often need to include them in sporting scenes.

Vehicles

Many people are still shy of including vehicles in their landscapes, maybe for aesthetic reasons, but more often because they are afraid of painting them. Whether we like it or not, vehicles are part of the environment and as such need to be included, on occasion, in our landscapes. It is important to be able to depict them with confidence and authenticity. They can also add movement to a picture, or place a landscape in a particular setting or period.

In rural scenes it is useful to be able to indicate tractors and agricultural machinery seen everywhere around farms. Old abandoned farm vehicles and tools, which can be found in yards and fields, are all part of the landscape and deserve to be included. Take bicycles as an example. They can give scale and movement to a painting, but do present their own difficulties. The only way to become proficient is to sketch them frequently, both being ridden and positioned stationary against walls. They are delicate looking objects which have a charm of their own and should be indicated loosely.

Trains, too, play their part in a landscape, and once you have grasped their basic shape and proportions, they can be blocked in with freedom. Bridges and viaducts over which they travel provide other painting possibilities, as do old signal boxes and stations.

Finally, one can still discover horse-drawn ploughs, carts and haywains, particularly in such places as the Amish regions of America, where religion forbids the use of motorised equipment. They can create a wistful motif and add a romantic notion to the art of the landscape painter.

The tractor is used as a device to lead the eye into the landscape. It also creates a narrative to the scene, suggesting man's relationship to the landscape.

Left, here John shows vehicles abandoned in the landscape. They no longer hold a practical purpose, but their elegant shapes create an interesting contrast to the surrounding fields.

Above, the canal has been used to divide the composition and the landscape. John combines blue pen and ink with watercolour to achieve this graphic style, where all elements are pared down to simple shapes and lines.

Index

N

O

P

Q

R

S

T

U

V

W

Acknowledgements

I would like to express my grateful thanks to Ann Mills, who has helped me enormously with the writing and Jenny Hickey who did all the typing from my almost indecipherable scribblings.

Ron Ranson

My great thanks, once again, to Ron Ranson for his faith in asking me to contribute a second book in his successful series – Ron Ranson's Painting School – and this time for sparing me the task of providing the text.

My thanks also to Jane Donovan, Senior Editor at Anaya, for her continuing advice and encouragement, to Jane Foster for her inspired planning and tolerance under pressure, and to Miranda Fellows who patiently listened to me and, with Ron, achieved a miracle of text.

I am greatly indebted to everyone involved, again not forgetting Doreen!

John Palmer